ELAPULTIEK

(WE ARE LOOKING TOWARDS)

shalan joudry

Pottersfield Press, Lawrencetown Beach, Nova Scotia, Canada

Copyright © 2019 shalan joudry

All rights reserved. No part of this publication may be reproduced or used or stored in any form or by any means – graphic, electronic or mechanical, including photocopying – or by any information storage or retrieval system without the prior written permission of the publisher. Any requests for photocopying, recording, taping or information storage and retrieval systems shall be directed in writing to the publisher or to Access Copyright, The Canadian Copyright Licensing Agency (www.AccessCopyright.ca). This also applies to classroom use.

Library and Archives Canada Cataloguing in Publication

Title: Elapultiek = We are looking towards ... / Shalan Joudry.
Names: Joudry, Shalan, 1979- author.
Identifiers: Canadiana (print) 20190046260 | Canadiana (ebook) 20190046511 | ISBN 9781988286662

  (softcover) | ISBN 9781988286679 (ebook)
Classification: LCC PS8619.O856 W4 2019 | DDC C812/.6—dc23

Cover painting by Melissa Labrador

Cover design by Gail LeBlanc

Pottersfield Press gratefully acknowledges the financial support of the Government of Canada through the Canada Book Fund for our publishing activities. We also acknowledge the support of the Canada Council for the Arts and the Province of Nova Scotia which has assisted us to develop and promote our creative industries for the benefit of all Nova Scotians.

Pottersfield Press
248 Leslie Road
East Lawrencetown, Nova Scotia, Canada, B2Z 1T4
Website: www.PottersfieldPress.com
To order, phone 1-800-NIMBUS9 (1-800-646-2879) www.nimbus.ca

Printed in Canada.

*for the Elders who led me here
and for the ecologists who sang with me*

Elapultiek was first produced by Two Planks and a Passion Theatre and opened at the Ross Creek Centre for the Arts in Canning, Nova Scotia, Mi'kma'ki, on August 25, 2018, with the following cast:

Natawintoq: shalan joudry
Bill: Matthew Lumley
With special guest: Robin Munro as the Wi'klatmuj
      (little forest person)
Director: Ken Schwartz
Drum Singer: shalan joudry
Stage Manager: Robin Munro
Dramaturge: Matthew Lumley

Wela'lioq

Wela'lin, Wskitqamu. May we remember how to be human things of the earth.

Wela'lin to Greg Turner for counting chimney swifts with me in downtown Bear River and for your friendship that ensued. Although the characters and plot are a work of fiction, the time we spent talking about our lives and the world around us inspired the concept of this story.

A special thank you to Albert Marshall for bringing the teaching of "two-eyed seeing," where we work with both our Indigenous cultural eye and mainstream science eye without one overpowering the other. As well, *wela'lin* for giving your blessing to share the story of Muin and the Seven Bird Hunters that Elders Lillian and Murdena Marshall revived with colleagues at Cape Breton University. *Wela'lioq* to the residential school survivors and Elders who tirelessly continue to teach and inspire the next generations.

Wela'lioq to the ecologists who work so dedicatedly to help the land, and especially to those who have opened their hearts to "two-eyed seeing." It's been a wonderful, hopeful journey.

Thank you to Matthew Lumley and Ken Schwartz for workshopping this script. I trusted that you both understood my vision and in turn you helped make this better. Thank you to Two Planks and a Passion Theatre and the Ross Creek Centre for the Arts for taking on this project and for taking good care of us throughout the work.

I'm appreciative of the funding from Environment and Climate Change Canada that sustained the Species at Risk work, which i'm thankful to have been part of for the past decade. Thank you to Arts NS for the funding that supported the writing of this piece as well as the touring of our first production. Thank you to Pottersfield Press for believing this performance story should also be shared in print form. *Wela'lin* to Melissa Labrador for the gorgeous image on the cover.

Wela'lin to my partner, Frank Meuse, who tended our home in my many absences during this project and was home to me in every way. Thank you to my daughters, Malaika and Milidow, whose laughter was always essential and their love for the world kept my hope burning when i wasn't sure how to fuel it.

Thank you to my mother, Sylvia Moore, and father, Steven Joudry, who both taught me to tell a good story.

Characters

Natawintoq (Nat) – early twenties, a Mi'kmaw drum singer from the local Mi'kmaw community.

Bill – mid fifties, a Euro-Nova Scotian biologist working for a research institute.

Scene 1

Meeting

(A camp fire in the middle of the woods close to an abandoned cabin with a tall brick chimney. Nat is tending the fire, dressed in a long cultural skirt. A smudge bowl and drum are close by. She sings a drum song before beginning.)

NAT: Wela'lioq. Wela'lioq to the earth, air, water, fire. Wela'lioq to the landscapes that influenced our history. Wela'lioq to all of the plants and animals who have made these lands what they are and continue to give up their lives to feed us. Wela'lioq to our ancestors, who survived incredible challenges and went on to birth new generations and passed on livelihoods so that we could be here today. Wela'lioq to not only the earth world but also the sky world. Thank you, Nakuset and Tepkunset, for lighting our way, day and night. And thank you, wela'lin to this fire. *(She makes an offering to the fire.)*

NAT: Grandmother, Nukumi, this isn't how I thought I would be starting my fast, without you. I hope wherever you are in the spirit world that you're taking care of Grandfather. What's my path? I need your help in this fast to find a vision.

BILL *(Calls from forest)*: Hello!

(Bill ENTERS with a pack and clipboard, startling Nat.)

BILL: Hi there. I didn't mean to frighten you. I'm a biologist with the research institute. I'm here to count the endangered chimney swifts. Sorry, again. It looks like I've disturbed your campfire. Looks cozy.

(Nat is silent.)

BILL: Have you seen the chimney swifts?

NAT: Excuse me?

BILL: Chimney swifts. *(Pulls out a guidebook from his pocket.)* Here. They're a small bird that nests and roosts in brick chimneys. They migrate and they're just coming back from the south, joining each night now in the chimneys before they pair up to mate and nest in a few weeks. *(Looks up to the sky.)* They come back to the roost at dusk. There's a few up there.

NAT: You can't be here right now.

BILL: I'm conducting research, with permission. I'm here tonight, and then four more times over the next month. Did I introduce myself? I'm Bill, and you are?

NAT: Nat.

BILL: As in Natalie?

NAT: No.

BILL: Okay, Nat.

NAT: When do you come back next?

BILL: In five days. I don't mean to push you out. You can stay. It's really quite remarkable. They come clustering in the sky more and more until the group of them is swarming in this circle and then at some point they all spiral down the chimney.

NAT: Yeah.

BILL: Off they go to feed a little longer. They'll all be back in a few minutes. What do you do, Nat? Are you in school?

NAT: I'm a singer.

BILL: What do you sing?

NAT: Drum songs.

BILL: You're an Aboriginal? Micmac?

NAT: Mi'kmaw. Yes.

BILL: Okay. Good for you.

NAT: There's some over there.

BILL: Yes. I'd say there's about thirty swifts in the group now. *(Looks to his clipboard.)* I didn't fill this in yet. Wind speed 3, I'd say. Cloud cover 40 percent. Temperature 17. State of chimney: weakened, possibly internally damaged.

NAT: What are you going to do with the papers?

BILL: Save the originals and copy them to send to the aerial insectivore specialists at Maritimes SwiftWatch. They coordinate the count nights.

NAT: Do you give the data back to the community here?

BILL: Other biologists do the stewardship part.

NAT: Then why are you at this spot, instead of just asking us in our community to do this? This is Mi'kmaw reserve land.

BILL: Actually, this is private land. The reserve boundary is right over there. This is where I come to monitor them. I speak with the landowner each spring to let him know I'll be here by his old cabin.

NAT: I was always told this was reserve until the river. My grandparents used to bring me here. We always camp –

BILL: The property boundary is over there. They're almost ready to dive in. I have to pay attention now.

(Silence.)

BILL: There we go. One!

(Bill jots on his papers. Nat looks to where the chimney/birds are.)

BILL: Two more ... ten, twenty, thirty, forty, fifty. Three. Wow, that was amazing. Two more.

NAT: There's three more.

BILL: They'll go in.

NAT: So this is all you do, count them and write it down?

BILL: There they go. Yes, I record the data and we

analyze them and discuss it all at recovery team meetings.

NAT: But all you do here is count them? I can do that so you don't have to. I'll call the SwiftWatch people and let them know. Maybe I can bring some youth and it can be a youth project.

BILL: That's quite all right. I have this covered.

NAT: Or we count and ask the Elders –

BILL: This is my job. I'm a biologist.

NAT: What's the definition of a biologist?

BILL: Someone who studies the living world.

NAT: In that case, I'm a biologist.

BILL: Also, usually that means someone who's formally trained in –

NAT: I would say my grandparents are biologists and my father, too.

BILL: *(Scoffs.)*

NAT: Nemultes, Bill!

(Nat EXITS.)

Scene 2

Counting Begins

BILL: Wind speed? I would say about a 1. Cloud cover 20 percent. Temperature 16 degrees.

(Nat ENTERS with safari clothes on.)

NAT: Metowlein, Bill?

BILL: Good evening, Nat. So we meet again.

NAT: E'he. Weli-wela'kw … Teke'k-ti. Kewji. Katu'ki'l? Epsin? Teknamuksin-ti. Peso'l. Ankapte'n koqowey ala'tu. *(Takes out her clipboard.)* I got the SwiftWatch forms.

BILL: You don't have all the data.

NAT: For last time? Yes I do. Sixty-three, wasn't it?

BILL: The protocol is to arrive a half-hour before dusk. You're late.

NAT: I was checking on them up the river.

(Both are preparing their notes.)

BILL: Did you take biology in high school, Nat?

NAT: Grade ten, yes. But I was also taught differently by Mi'kmaw Elders and woodspeople.

BILL: Oh?

NAT: Elders taught me that some of what you call "non-living" are actually animate things to us. Like how we call sweatlodge rocks grandfathers because of their energy.

BILL: Science gives us an objective view.

NAT: Objective? The science you were taught finds its roots in European worldview and history. I studied Mi'kmaw biology.

BILL: Mi'kmaw biology?

NAT: It's all about relationships. Our word for the swifts is kaktukopnji'jk. I'm not sure exactly the English translation, something about thunders or fire.

BILL: In Latin it's *chaetura pelagica*. *Chaetura* from Greek meaning long flowing hair or tail. And *pelagica* is Latin origin for marine.

NAT: That doesn't make any sense. I don't think this is the best direction to see them go in. There's a shadow there and that other tree is in the way of the swoop.

(Nat moves.)

NAT: I think it's better from over here.

BILL: No, as the light lowers you'll be looking right into the glare and the birds will be difficult to focus on. Here is best.

NAT: I'll stay over here just in case.

BILL: Suit yourself.

(They both prepare.)

NAT: I came over last night and sang for them, for the forest and all the critters. I thought this place needed some more positive energy.

(Silence.)

BILL: One. *(Writes it down.)*

NAT: Oh! But those ones didn't go in. They're still flying. I guess they aren't ready for bed.

BILL: I've been coming to this spot for years and I can tell you there's no negative energy here.

NAT: I can hear them chattering.

BILL: I would also caution you against anthropomorphizing the birds. They aren't people; they're birds. And we need to think of their habits and communication through the lens of being birds, not people.

NAT: They're spiralling.

(The swifts descend into the chimney while Bill and Nat count over each other's numbers.)

BILL: Three in. Ten, twenty, thirty, forty, fifty, sixty. Three. Five more.

NAT: Four ... Twelve ... Eighteen ... Twenty-nine ... Forty-one ... Forty-five ... Fifty-two ... Fifty-nine ... Sixty-eight ... Seventy-three.

BILL: Seventy-one. *(Writes.)*

NAT: *(Writes.)* I counted seventy-three over here.

BILL: There were two that looked like they went in, but they flew on behind that branch there instead.

NAT: Yeah, not those two.

(Bill looks down to write.)

NAT: Another one.

BILL: *(Looks up, waits.)* Three.

NAT: Did you get that other one?

BILL: I got all of them.

NAT: If you say so.

BILL: One bird here or there in the flurry isn't the point. We're doing our best to estimate, as long as we're being consistent with our counting from one session to the next and from one year to the next.

NAT: As long as you're in control, right?

BILL: I'm just doing my job. Two more. *(Writes.)*

NAT: Maybe we can do this species at risk work by using our cultural practices.

BILL: One. That might have been the last one. Now we wait the fifteen minutes to make sure it really was the last one. I'm not sure what you're suggesting. Cultural activities?

NAT: We were left out of so much for so long. Maybe we have our own ideas. And some people in my community live in poverty while you make a salary standing on our land.

BILL: I hear there are going to be a lot more programs for natives.

NAT: Mi'kmaq. Or L'nu'k. Say the nation you mean in the territory where you mean it or "Indigenous" if you're talking about all over Turtle Island or North America. And "programs"? You don't get it.

BILL: Then explain it to me.

NAT: I'm tired of explaining it. I was raised by my grandparents. I grew up watching them work hard to find the light in the forest floor. And now me, my life has been spent calling these things out.

BILL: Perhaps you attract that extra work.

NAT: I've always had more work. I've had to learn the Euro-Canadian English way, but then also learn from my Elders about what it means to be L'nu. The onus is always on us to walk both worlds.

BILL: I have to learn the scientific names and the common names of species.

NAT: Where do your ancestors come from?

BILL: Most of my family are of British descent. Some came off the boats into the New England states in the sixteen and seventeen hundreds. I do have one grandmother who arrived in Nova Scotia direct from Scotland.

NAT: The weird thing is that so many people identify this landscape with Scottish culture, the plaid and fiddle music, rather than Mi'kmaw language and culture.

BILL: The European settlers made Nova Scotia what it is today.

NAT: As well as the Mi'kmaq. You must understand that, right?

BILL: Are you saying that we can't celebrate our history?

NAT: This land is overflowing with European-Canadian celebrations, statues, and plaques. We should take some down and make some new ones, accurate ones and Mi'kmaw ones.

BILL: We can't erase history.

NAT: It's not about erasing history. It's about not celebrating the atrocities, telling a more accurate history, and honouring Mi'kmaw ancestors and not just the European colonial ones. It's about taking some of these historical genocidal leaders off their pedestals. I was at the rally in Kjipuktuk over the weekend and we said the –

BILL: What's that?

NAT: You call it Halifax.

BILL: Oh, okay. Halifax.

NAT: It was called Kjipuktuk long before the Europeans came over and renamed it. The offensive leaders just need to come down off their pedestals. If people want a statue for them maybe make them like this. *(She stands in various poses.)* Or like this. Not like this with their arms blazing and cape flying. And where are all the Mi'kmaw statues to celebrate this landscape that they took care of and welcomed the first few ships of newcomers, hey? You wouldn't even be here if it weren't for those Mi'kmaw ancestors.

BILL: I try to stay out of politics.

NAT: Lucky you. To be born Indigenous is to be born into politics and these conversations, whether we want to carry them or not.

(Beat/pause of silence.)

NAT: When did the last one go in?

BILL: You need a watch.

(Beat.)

BILL: I don't know my old English or Scottish culture.

NAT: You can go back to England or Scotland to find whatever you're looking for. This here is the homeland of the Mi'kmaq and nowhere else do they speak our language or hold our culture safe. Only here: Mi'kma'ki.

BILL: There goes another swift. I guess we have to restart the clock. *(Beat.)* Another fifteen minutes. *(Beat.)* It's okay if you need to go home.

NAT: This is home.

BILL: Fine.

Scene 3

Wi'klatmuj

BILL: I wasn't sure you were coming back.

NAT: Tet.

BILL: Ready for another count night?

NAT: E'he. Katu ki'l?

BILL: I assume ay-hay means yes.

NAT: E'he.

BILL: There, I've learned a word in your language.

NAT: As you should. It's the first human language of this land.

BILL: Cloudy, 100 percent cover, but not raining.

NAT: I don't see or hear any swifts.

BILL: No.

(Silence.)

BILL: I brought a video camera tonight in case you did come. I thought maybe you could be in charge of getting the video for me. I'll check the count on slow motion later. *(Hands her a video camera.)*

NAT: Sure. I'll verify your data.

BILL: Well, I'll take it home and watch it.

(Silence.)

NAT: I had a few youth out here last night. They had a great time.

BILL: You came an extra night?

NAT: Yeah. It was really wonderful.

BILL: Did you count them?

NAT: No. We just enjoyed watching them. And then we sang a friendship song.

(Silence.)

BILL: Geologists say that these hills of the Appalachian were once as high as the Rockies. And since, over all that time, they've slowly eroded, worn away so that they're now only hills. Incredible. Just think: we humans have been on this earth for such a short amount of time by comparison. What's great about talking about the science of the landscape is that it renders cultural differences moot.

NAT: The mountains and rocks are the oldest and wisest. That's why our Elders teach us to call them grandfathers and grandmothers.

BILL: I'm not sure how wise a mountain is.

NAT: Why do you have to be so oppositional to everything I say and believe?

BILL: It's you who is being confrontational. You've been passive-aggressive since the day we met.

NAT: I'm here for the swifts. I still don't see any.

BILL: There's a chance that the swifts didn't even leave the roost this morning if it was raining, or they went in early today because of it.

NAT: They might be in the roost right now?

BILL: It's possible.

NAT: Then why aren't we going over to check?

BILL: I'm starting with protocols first.

NAT: I'll go over and check. Oh, and please don't touch these things here.

(Nat EXITS. Bill shuffles, looking over at Nat's things.)

(Nat ENTERS.)

NAT: Yup. They're in there already. I heard them chattering like when they're flying. I wonder what they're telling each other. Maybe where the good food is or tips on where to go tomorrow.

(Bill puts his things down.)

BILL: I'll go have a listen and be right back. Please watch the sky, just in case.

NAT: Obviously.

(Nat watches sky and hums while Bill EXITS briefly. Bill ENTERS.)

BILL: Yup, they're in there already. The count is over tonight. *(Examining his things.)* Hey, where's my clipboard?

NAT: You know, that reminds me of a joke I heard.

BILL: What?

NAT: What do you call a deer with no eyes?

BILL: What?

NAT: No-i-deer.

BILL: What?

NAT: Koqowe?

BILL: You want me to go away?

NAT: Mo'qwe. Koqowe means what.

BILL: Are we having a conversation?

NAT: I know I am. I'm not sure about you.

BILL: Back to the beginning. Do you know where my clipboard is?

NAT: Mo'qwe. No-i-deer.

BILL: I must have dropped it.

NAT: Etukjel. Or a wi'klatmu'j might have taken it. Probably thought you were writing down forest secrets.

BILL: A what?

NAT: A wi'klatmu'j. A little forest person.

BILL: Like fairies and leprechauns?

NAT: Similar, yeah.

BILL: So you're telling me the Little People took my clipboard?

NAT: Not little people. Person. One. It just takes one to run off with something like that.

(Bill looks around.)

BILL: Did you see anyone?

NAT: Mo'qwe. I was looking for renegade swifts. *(Silence.)* Hey, what do you call a deer with no eyes and no legs?

(Silence.)

NAT: Still no-i-deer.

BILL: This is ridiculous. Fairies don't exist and you singing to the trees or speaking in code talk doesn't do anything to help protect these species. I'm just trying to get my observations. It might just be a game for you but this is my life's work here.

NAT: Good luck with that.

(Nat EXITS.)

Scene 4

Contested Land and a Raccoon

(Bill prepares, holding a new notebook.)

BILL: Wind speed 2. Cloud cover 1 percent. Beautiful sky.

(Nat ENTERS loaded with Mi'kmaw items. She sets up an elaborate cultural practice to begin the count night.)

NAT: Kwe', Bill.

(Nat continues to set up.)

BILL: What are you doing?

NAT: Before we do this count, it's important to start with an opening ceremony.

BILL: Good grief.

NAT: I'm going to sing a welcome song first to the beat of the drum, remind us of our heartbeat. And then we'll smudge our gear. Don't worry, I'll help you.

BILL: No thank you. *(Nat hands him an item.)* Actually, I don't really appreciate you forcing me into this ceremony. *(Nat begins drumming.)* If you need to do something like this, I suggest you do it at home or before you come up the path.

NAT: I'm sorry, Bill, this is Mi'kmaw reserve land here and I feel that a ceremony is needed. If you don't like it, then you can remove yourself until I'm done.

BILL: No. Al Johnson and I just made an agreement. This is going to be my land.

NAT: What?

BILL: Al's agreed to sell it to me.

NAT: This is our community land.

BILL: In a few weeks it will be mine. And I will protect the roost and the trees. It's a good thing.

NAT: You can't buy it.

BILL: The municipality and Mr. Johnson say I can. And therefore if I ask that there be no ceremony, then I'd like you to adhere to my request, as my guest here.

NAT: I won't allow you to buy this land. I don't know how, but I'll think of something. I'll do a hunger strike or move in – that's it, I'll just stay here. This is my spot.

BILL: I really don't understand why being Mi'kmaw makes you so sensitive and you go right for the dramatic standoff.

NAT: I can't believe –

BILL: There's a raccoon on the chimney!

(They both look.)

BILL: It's just sitting there.

NAT: The swifts won't be able to get in!

BILL: We have to scare it down.

NAT: How? Throw something?

BILL: No. Maybe yell.

(They both yell.)

NAT: Ohh. Don't just look at us and then lay back down, you punk.

BILL: And here come the swifts.

NAT: What are they going to do?

BILL: We're going to find out.

NAT: What if I climb up there and non-violently ask the raccoon to leave?

BILL: Sounds like a broken bone to me. I can't have that liability on my clock.

NAT: But these are our kaktukopnji'jk! Get away, you bandit. Shoo!

BILL: No one's diving in.

NAT: Then go somewhere else, you guys.

BOTH: Oh.

BILL: That one tried to go in.

NAT: One just did.

BILL: Ten, twenty, thirty, forty …

NAT: The raccoon just went in after them.

BILL: Four, two.

NAT: Five just came out.

BILL: Ten in.

NAT: Ten, twenty, thirty, forty out. Look, the raccoon came out. Is she licking her lips? Ooh, you killer.

BILL: How many are left in the chimney? You got the outs and I have ... *(Checks tally)* fifty-seven in.

NAT: Forty-five came out.

BILL: Twelve still in there.

(Silence.)

BILL: I'll come back tomorrow night just to check and see if the raccoon comes back.

NAT: I'll come, too. Maybe I'll bring something louder.

BILL: I'm not sure being louder will distract this one.

NAT: We have to try something.

BILL: I know.

(Bill goes to exit.)

NAT: Bill, don't buy this land.

BILL: See you tomorrow.

(Nat tends to the fire and Bill EXITS.)

Scene 5

Roost Check

(Bill ENTERS and prepares. Nat ENTERS with extra gear.)

NAT: I'm ready for you tonight, Amaljukwej!

BILL: Hi, Nat. Let's not argue tonight.

NAT: I'd like to tell you what I've decided.

BILL: Yes?

NAT: You say you've been working on species at risk for many years but from what I can tell the situation isn't getting much better. It seems that all you do is measure things. I sat and talked with the fire, which is my methodology –

BILL: That's not a –

NAT: I've decided that I won't count the swifts with you tonight. You can do that with your mainstream eye, but what I need to do is use our cultural teachings.

BILL: That's what I've been saying: let me do the biology work.

NAT: I'll need you to count in your head because I need silence.

BILL: Fine.

NAT: Good.

(Both look to the sky. Some birds are trickling in, Bill makes notes. Silence.)

BILL: How do you think we know when to list species as being at risk?

NAT: You pay attention.

BILL: No one is observant enough to know all the species and their relative abundance and relationship to threat.

NAT: My family still spends a lot of time on the land.

BILL: You still live in houses and drive in vehicles, I assume. We all live a little less connected. We count them. Biologists count the population, map them, and then make recommendations when they seem low. Like these birds. There they go.

(They watch the birds funnel in the chimney. Nat is in an active listening stance.)

BILL: I think that's all of them.

(Nat comes out of her stance. Bill counts his tally.)

BILL: We're down seventeen.

NAT: They're in crisis. They need two things.

BILL: Oh yeah?

NAT: We need to offer tobacco to the fire to send them hope.

BILL: That's not a recovery action.

NAT: If you take time to humble yourself and talk to the fire, you'll find it helps the work. Try it. You'll see.

BILL: What's the other thing they need?

NAT: We need to hold a public meeting in town to get everyone involved.

BILL: We just need to stick to the count and make recovery plans. Stewardship and citizen science are blown out of proportion. "I Love Swifts" buttons aren't going to help.

NAT: I'm going to organize it.

(Silence.)

BILL: If there is going to be any kind of discussion about the species, then I should be there.

NAT: Okay, then come.

BILL: I still didn't find my data sheets from the beginning of the season. I need to send them in to Maritimes Swiftwatch.

(Silence.)

BILL: You don't know what happened to my clipboard, do you?

NAT: Mo'qwe. Of course not.

BILL: Just asking.

Scene 6

Community Meeting

(Bill and Nat are in the middle of their community meeting. Bill has just explained the background information about the chimney swifts.)

BILL: Finding communal roost sites is challenging for this species as nowadays we hardly give forests the time to mature ecologically. All of that is just one part of their struggle. Other issues are in their southern wintering grounds and also studies suggest their food sources now no longer provide them with the right nutrients they once did.

NAT: Thank you, Bill. That was great information. Now we're ready to share and discuss where to go from here on this project.

BILL: I can answer questions. Nat, why don't you get the question box.

(Nat holds the box.)

NAT: Fine. Thank you to everyone for writing down your questions and ideas. *(Pulls a card out.)* The first one asks, "If I have swifts in my chimney, am I allowed to clean the chimney in the spring and fall as I normally do?" *(Pulls out another card.)*

BILL: Yes. We just ask that you don't make fires or clean your chimneys during the season they are here.

NAT: Oh, this one's important.

BILL: Okay, what's the question?

NAT: What is the Mi'kmaw name for chimney swifts?

BILL: Right. Why don't you answer this, Nat.

NAT: Kaktukopnji'jk. Kak-tu-kopn-ji'jk. *(She pronounces it for everyone.)*

BILL: Thank you, Nat.

NAT: Yes, I thought that would be a good question to put in. *(She pulls out another card.)*

BILL: It might be a good time to mention the Latin –

NAT: Bill, this one should be next.

(Nat passes it to Bill.)

BILL: "You conservationists don't care about the town. We need to make a living, too. There's enough birds in the world." Interesting comments and concerns. We do understand that we need to have balance between human development and the rest of the ecosystem needs. However, we have well over thirty terrestrial species at risk in southern Nova Scotia alone. That's telling us something.

NAT: These birds are our messengers. They show us that we're no longer in balance with nature.

(Nat looks at another card.)

BILL: That's right, Nat. And to the person who wrote that comment: I do appreciate the honesty in sharing your views.

NAT: Who wrote this one? You're being ignorant against me and my community. Who wrote this one? Who? I'm trying to help this land. My grandfather knew you guys in town were racist and nothing's ever changed.

(Nat EXITS. Bill picks up the card and reads it, then EXITS.)

Scene 7

Just a Biologist

(Nat is tending the fire. Bill ENTERS.)

BILL: Listen, Nat, I'm so sorry about the last card. But there were some really great comments and some donations towards the swift work.

NAT: That wasn't the kind of community meeting I first had in mind. We should have sat in a circle and shared thoughts. That way everyone is equal in the room. And for something so serious you have to let people settle into the space together. That's why we do openings.

BILL: We had the comment box so that everyone had the opportunity to share.

NAT: It doesn't replace our methods of how to meet and listen to each other. How are we going to protect and recover species at risk without this being the work and conversation of everyone?

BILL: I don't think it would help the swifts anyway. But if I buy this land and cabin, then I will be able to handle this.

NAT: Don't. This land is part of our reserve. We don't have much land left that we can call ours and govern ourselves on.

BILL: It's for conservation, though.

NAT: Usually conservation means non-Indigenous people draw a boundary around an area and say no people allowed. Is that what you mean?

BILL: I guess it depends on what it's for. Right now I'm just thinking about the chimney swifts.

NAT: Can't you think about the people, too?

BILL: I'm just a biologist.

(Silence.)

BILL: Have a good winter.

(Bill EXITS.)

Scene 8

Astronomy with a Bear Story

[THE FOLLOWING SPRING]

NAT: Happy Siwkw. Happy Spring.

(Nat sings a welcome song for the swifts. Bill ENTERS during the song but doesn't interrupt her.)

NAT: Bill.

BILL: Nat. You're here early.

NAT: So are you.

BILL: Wind speed ... 1 ... Cloud cover ... 5 percent ... Temperature ... 18 ... State of chimney ... –

NAT: Worn out, crooked, on stolen land.

BILL: Are you counting tonight or are you still anti-science?

NAT: I don't think the numbers matter as much as understanding how they are doing.

BILL: Do you want to know if their nesting season was successful last year and if their population rebounded from the raccoon? Those are numbers.

(Nat pauses.)

NAT: I'll know.

BILL: Okay.

NAT: My father and I watch the swifts when he fishes the North Branch Stream a few kilometres inland. When I was a kid there were more swifts in this chimney. They also disappeared from the chimney in the old school.

BILL: You didn't tell me you knew about the swifts before I met you.

NAT: You never asked. My grandparents used to say that in the olden days once these birds were here it meant the sea trout, salmon, and gaspereau were on their way and it was time to be at the summer camp on the shore.

BILL: Anecdotes are good as reference. It still doesn't answer all of our questions.

NAT: We pass on qualitative information through our stories and language. That's our way of sharing sciences and vetting through the generations. I can teach about astronomy simply by telling a story about a bear.

BILL: Stories aren't science.

NAT: Wanna bet?

(Silence.)

BILL: Sure.

NAT: If I can demonstrate lessons in astronomy with my bear story, then you have to sing a Mi'kmaw chant with me. And –

BILL: That's enough. Okay. If you don't prove your point, you will have to let me count the swifts in peace.

NAT: What do you mean "in peace"?

BILL: No drumming.

(Pauses.)

NAT: Okay. Prepare yourself.

(Nat stretches her gaze and arms across the night sky.)

NAT: Lillian Marshall and Murdena Marshall tell the story about the night sky. We look to the north before dawn to see this story. You'll recognize the four stars there as the Big Dipper, but we call it Muin, Bear.

In the spring, this is where Muin is, poised this way, as she's climbing down from her winter den looking for food. But Muin isn't the only one who's hungry and following her are three more stars. We call those the Bird Hunters. There are also a fourth, fifth, sixth, and seventh Bird Hunter. Every morning when you look to the sky, you'll see that Muin and the Hunters have shifted a bit across the sky. All summer long they chase Muin across the sky.

By the fall the last Hunters lose the trail. Actually, it's because the four stars have fallen below the horizon and you can't see them anymore. When it's just the first three left, they finally catch Muin, shoot her, and she rises up on her hind legs, bleeding a great deal. She dies and her spirit leaves. The first Bird Hunter jumps on her body and gets covered in blood. He shakes it from his feathers sending blood splattering all over the maple trees and they turn red. Then it is late fall and the first three Bird Hunters begin the work to cook Muin's body. The other four Bird Hunters finally regain the trail, after all the work was done, and they share in the feast.

By the winter, Muin's skeleton is on its back this way, directly above you in the night sky. In the midwinter when we see the stars this way, it reminds us to give thanks to those who give their lives to sustain us through the winter.

After the winter is over Muin's spirit enters a new bear sleeping in her den and the story restarts. In our culture we teach how all life is cyclical and so by the spring, here she is getting ready to climb out of her winter den again. That's not just a fun story, but a way to know the calendar by looking to the stars and seeing where we are in the story. As you follow along through the year, you will notice that the bigger story of Muin and the Seven Bird Hunters rotate every day and every year in the pattern. The story rotates around one star, a star that you could also set your bearings by.

(Silence.)

NAT: So, Bill, where would that star be?

(Bill reluctantly points.)

BILL: That would be the North Star.

NAT: We call it Tatapn. Our ancestors had to teach the young to know the signals of the land and light. People remember better through story and so you turn everything into characters and plot, imbedding the science in there. Our stories are about natural patterns told in a holistic way.

BILL: Hmm.

NAT: And so ... I think you owe me something, maybe a song?

BILL: Here come the swifts.

Scene 9

The Fire

[A FEW DAYS LATER]

(Nat is studying the cabin location.)

NAT: Who would do this?

(Bill ENTERS.)

BILL: I came as soon as I heard.

(Both stare at the rubble.)

NAT: Everything burned. Even the chimney was pushed over.

BILL: It's all gone.

(Silence.)

NAT: The swifts were already out, but now they have nowhere to go. Do you think someone was upset after the town meeting last year and did this for spite?

BILL: We won't know. I'll speak with Al and see what he thinks.

NAT: You don't think he burned it because of the attention, do you?

BILL: Probably not, seeing as I was going to buy the place.

NAT: Bill.

BILL: I know, I know, it's reserve land anyway. I just meant I don't think Al would want to see the place ruined.

NAT: Did you just say it's reserve land?

BILL: Yes.

NAT: You believe me?

BILL: Yes.

NAT: Good. Finally you side with oral tradition instead of data.

BILL: Actually, I found data.

NAT: What do you mean?

BILL: I looked into it at the lands registry and found that about a hundred years ago someone took the liberty to survey off this part of the reserve and make a private sale. I'm not sure if it was intentional or accidental.

NAT: When did you find that out?

BILL: In the winter.

NAT: What?

BILL: There's nothing we can do, Nat. It's been resold seven times and re-parcelled into a larger plot. It's in the jurisdiction of private lands now. Maybe the community can buy back other lands to make up for the lost hectares.

NAT: We're not going to rebuy our own lands. How could you not even tell me that you found this out?

BILL: I didn't mean to keep it from you.

NAT: It sounds like you were keeping it from me. Why? Because you wanted to buy it before I made it a larger issue?

BILL: No!

NAT: We have to show this to the municipal authorities to have this righted.

BILL: I don't think that will solve this. What's done is done.

NAT: Are you saying you won't help us? I thought you stood for good things, important things. You have to help me.

BILL: I can't get involved.

NAT: Why not?

BILL: I'm not into that, Nat. I don't want to end up on TV siding with a bunch of –

NAT: A bunch of what? Mi'kmaq?

BILL: Activists.

NAT: We have to do everything we can to right the wrongs, for other species and other people.

BILL: I can't handle more than one cause right now. Look at this rubble and what I now have to deal with. I've dedicated my life for species at risk. I've been working double time for the past two years, spending days away from my home, going to the field to collect more data, analyzing it in the middle of the night and preparing presentations for governments and conferences trying to make a difference for a species before I retire. I wanted to buy this land and build chimney swift towers that finally work and grow the population. We could recover this species. That was supposed to be my legacy. How can I do that now? You're too young to understand. This is all I had left.

NAT: All you wanted was make a name for yourself? I had no idea you were so selfish.

BILL: You're selfish. I don't think you're really here for the swifts at all. You're just trying to destabilize anything that's not Mi'kmaw.

NAT: That's not true.

BILL: I'm sorry that nations fight and your ancestors happened to lose the war here.

NAT: They didn't lose. Those treaties were about sharing territory and having two jurisdictions for both Europeans and Mi'kmaq to be governed their own ways. How can you stand there defending a species from going extinct but then expect my culture can go extinct and that's okay? Stop telling me I have to assimilate.

BILL: Stop forcing your culture on me.

NAT: But then why do we have to conform to yours to make everyone happy?

BILL: I'm done with this conversation.

(Bill EXITS.)

Scene 10

Hopeless or Hope

(Nat is at the fire.)

NAT: Nukumi, I don't understand. I followed my heart. I trusted. I worked. How did we end up here with everything broken? How can fire both give life and take it away? Did I not follow the right path?

(She attempts to sing a drum song but ends abruptly. She slumps down. Bill ENTERS with a camera and takes a picture of the rubble.)

NAT: Go away.

BILL: Nat? What are you still doing here?

NAT: I don't want to see you. I'm doing a fast.

BILL: Are you okay?

NAT: What do you care? It doesn't matter. I give up. Happy now? You can do whatever science you want and watch it do nothing.

BILL: Nat.

NAT: The world is already in ruins. Humans are destroying everything around us. I'm done.

BILL: You're just a kid.

NAT: You don't know how much I've already fought. Sometimes that broken, pushed-down tree can only fight for so long until fungus finally takes its toll and the tree goes back to soil. You don't know what it's like to be part of the least favourable statistic category in the country. Young Indigenous woman.

BILL: You're not a statistic.

NAT: I am a statistic. Just when you think there's hope, another storm comes and pushes the tree further. Maybe some things are just meant to disappear.

BILL: Even after a storm devastates a forest, the trees keep growing. Even bent over, a tree will use a branch as the new top. You just need to focus on the positive.

NAT: You're up there in the canopy because we were mowed over long ago. Now you're the ones enjoying all the sun and probably drinking all the nutrients in the soil, telling us below to be happy we're not dead. And those of us who survived were stripped of their bark and heartwood.

BILL: Are you talking about residential schools? That was long ago.

NAT: My mother can't hug me or tell me she loves me, because her parents found that hard, because they went to residential school. It all still affects us. Our language. I'm seen as less L'nu because we lost our language. No. We didn't lose it. It was taken on purpose, beat out of us.

(Silence.)

BILL: You should go home and get some rest.

NAT: Leave me alone.

(Nat goes to get firewood and finds something on the ground.)

NAT: Isn't this your clipboard?

(Bill takes it.)

BILL: I'll come check on you tomorrow.

(Bill EXITS. Nat looks toward the rubble.)

NAT: We failed you. This was my job and I failed you. Mskey. I'm so sorry, kaktukopnji'jk.

(Nat slumps, crying, and falls asleep. Bill ENTERS and checks on Nat.)

NAT: Nukumi?

BILL: It's me, Bill.

(Nat doesn't respond. He looks to the fire and moves over to it.)

BILL: Hi, fire. I'm not sure what to say. I work on species at risk. It's challenging, almost hopeless, just watching species disappear. There have been days that I've wanted to give up, find something else that's less depressing, or where I can see change. And now Nat. I can't answer these things either. How am I supposed to make up for what my ancestors did to her ancestors? And is that even fair to put on my shoulders, because I don't know how to fix things or how to help her community. But she sure is a spitfire, sure of what she wants and why. I used to be like that for this work. Maybe I'm getting tired, too.

(Nat stirs, listens to Bill towards the end. She raises up, collects her drum, and slowly sings a healing song.)

NAT: My name is Natawintoq: she sings.

BILL: It suits you.

(Something startles them and they look around the sky.)

NAT: I know that sound. Swifts. Where are they? There. Why are you back? There's no chimney. Bill, look.

BILL: Oh wow. And they're swirling.

NAT: E'he.

(Both gasp and they are silent as they watch swifts descend.)

NAT: A tree? They found an old tree over there.

BILL: A tree.

NAT: That wasn't that many of them, twenty-ish. Bill, do we have to count?

BILL: No.

NAT: They found an old tree. Do you think they were going in there the whole time and we just never noticed?

BILL: Actually, look at the very top edge of it. That looks freshly broken off.

NAT: The thunderstorm must have broken it. The Thunders. Ha. They found a new home. I'm glad our community hasn't been cutting those old trees. My grandparents were part of protecting places like this. They said it was a place for ceremony.

BILL: I've got something for you.

(Bill goes to his pack and removes a large envelope.)

BILL: In here is all the data that I have about the surveying and mis-selling of the land. I think you should take it to your Band Council.

(Bill hands her the envelope. Nat looks through it.)

NAT: Wela'lin, Bill.

BILL: What else do you need?

NAT: I need you to listen without being defensive. We need to be heard.

BILL: Okay. Rest up and see you again soon.

NAT: E'he.

Scene 11

Celebration

[THE FOLLOWING SPRING]

NAT: Happy Siwkw. Happy Spring.

BILL: I see your medicines and drum. Are you still thinking you might do a fast?

NAT: I'll wait to find an Elder to host me a good way. Maybe next summer. I've decided to return to university this fall to finish my Bachelor of Arts in Music.

BILL: Natawintoq, that's really great.

NAT: An Elder reminded me recently to thank you.

BILL: For what?

NAT: We are grateful that you and other ecologists work so hard to help the land. We need more people to watch out for nature and be a voice. Thank you.

BILL: Are you ready to begin?

NAT: Thank you, wela'lioq to the earth and landscape, this geology of mountains and rivers. Wela'lioq to the plants and animals who made this place livable. We give thanks to all human ancestors around the world who survived incredible odds and passed on teachings about their world they knew. We stand here wanting to give thanks to the Thunders and Old Forests who have taken care of so many critters who call you home. Wela'lioq to the kaktukopnjij'jk, the swifts, like us Mi'kmaq who are struggling to survive the changing world. Thank you for giving us a reason.

(Nat picks up a music maker/ji'kmaqn.)

NAT: Okay, Bill, I didn't forget that I won the bet. You're going to sing a Mi'kmaw chant with me.

(She hands it to Bill.)

BILL: All right.

NAT: We're going to sing a friendship song to welcome back the swifts.

(Nat teaches him a friendship song.)

NAT: Here they are.

(Looking at the new site, the old tree, Bill takes his notes and counts as they watch the swifts. Nat continues to sing another round of the friendship song.)

BILL: Thirty-six.

NAT: Thirty-eight.

(Pauses.)

BILL: Okay. Thirty-eight.

NAT: Msit No'kmaq.

Translations

Please note that the Mi'kmaw words and phrases i used in this script are pronounced and written only as i have learned and remembered them. I acknowledge that there are other variations in dialect and orthography. Here is how i say them and understand them:

Amaljukwej (a-mahl-joo-gwech) – raccoon

Ankapte'n koqowey ala'tu (ahn-gap-dehn go-ho-way ah-lah-doo) – look what I have

E'he (eh-hey) – yes

Elapultiek (eh-lah-bool-dee-egg) – we are looking at/towards

Epsin? (ehp-sin) – Are you hot?

Etukjel (eh-dook-jel) – maybe

Ji'kmaqn (jeeg-mah-hn) – a split ash instrument played like wooden spoons

Kaktukopnji'jk (gahg-doo-go-boon-jeej-k) – chimney swifts

Katu'ki'l (gah-doo-geel) – What about you?

Kewji (gow-chee) – I'm cold.

Kjipuktuk (uhk-jee-book-took) – Mi'kmaw traditional encampment area now called Halifax

Koqowe (go-ho-way) – what

Kwe' (gway) – hi

L'nu (ool-noo) – Indigenous person, and interchangeable with "Mi'kmaw"

L'nu'k (ool-noog) – Indigenous people and interchangeable with "Mi'kmaq"

Metowlein? (meh-dow-lane) – How are you?

Mi'kma'ki (meeg-mah-ghee) – Traditional territory of the Mi'kmaq

Mi'kmaq (meeg-mahq) – Indigenous people of the Mi'kmaw nation

Mi'kmaw (meeg-mah) – Indigenous person of the Mi'kmaw nation; also used as an adjective

Mo'qwe (moe-h-way) – no

Msit No'kmaq (m-sit noe-g-mah) – all my relations

Mskey (ms-gae) – sorry

Muin (moo-in) – bear

Nakuset (nah-goo-set) – Sun

Natawintoq (nada-win-dohq) – s/he sings

Nemultes (ne-mool-dehs) – See you later.

Nukumi (noo-goom-ee) – my grandmother

Peso'l (beh-sohl) – I can smell you.

Siwkw (seew-gw) – Spring

Tatapn (dada-bn) – North Star

Teke'k-ti (deh-geh-g-dee) – It's a bit chilly.

Teknamuksin-ti (deh-gn-nah-moog-sin-dee) – You're sweating a bit.

Tepkunset (dep-goon-set) – Moon

Tet – Here

Wela'lin (weh-lah-lyn) – "thank you" to singular

Wela'lioq (weh-lah-lee-oh) – "thank you" to plural

Weli-wela'kw (well-ee-weh-lah-gw) – good evening

Wi'klatmuj (weeg-lad-ah-mooj) – trickster character, like the "Little People" of the forest

Wskitqamu (oo-sgeed-ha-moo) – Earth

Kaktukopnji'jk (Chimney Swifts)

The chimney swift is a threatened species in Canada and an endangered species within Nova Scotia. It is a small (twelve to fourteen centimetres) bird with narrow, pointed wings that curve backwards to form a bow-and-arrow silhouette. You will see chimney swifts feeding in the sky not too far from rivers before dusk. The chimney swift's legs are very short and do not support its body weight for walking or perching, so the swift remains "on the wing" all day from dawn until dusk. In its roost or nest site in the evening, the chimney swift clings to the side of the substrate using its specially adapted feet, and its spiny tail acts as a brace.

These birds migrate between their northern breeding habitats and their overwintering grounds in South America. When they arrive in our territory in early or mid May the birds will find communal roosting sites before they separate in pairs to nest through the forest. Before European colonization in Mi'kma'ki, these birds were roosting in large, old, hollowed-out trees. They later found brick and stone chimneys were excellent locations for roosting and nesting sites as they could cling to the rough sides and nest fairly easily. With the modernization of home heating to eliminate wood- and coal-burning fireplaces, chimneys are being capped and metal-lined, or demolished. Together with the dwindling presence of large mature trees, the loss of the chimney swifts' habitat presents a challenge for their populations. Recent research also suggests that an increase in pesticide use and decrease in insect prey is also a large factor in the chimney swift decline.

Maritimes SwiftWatch manages the volunteer program that identifies chimney swift nest and roost sites, works with landowners to maintain swift-friendly properties, and monitors swift populations in New Brunswick and Nova Scotia. In order to avoid double-counting swifts as they move between roost sites, the count nights are co-ordinated so that every roost is monitored on the same dates in May and early June each year. Ecologists and volunteers in each community where a communal roost has been noted are asked to estimate the numbers of swifts that descend into the roost sites, using a standard protocol. This work helps Maritimes SwiftWatch calculate the population fluctuations across the region and over time. Additional monitoring over the summer months helps ecologists understand the relative importance of each roost site to swifts throughout the breeding and migration periods, and also helps demonstrate the value of this habitat to landowners hosting these roost sites. To learn more about chimney swifts and the SwiftWatch program, please visit: https://www.birdscanada.org/volunteer/ai/chsw/

Etuaptmumk ("Two-Eyed Seeing")

It was Elder Albert Marshall from Eskasoni, Unama'ki (Cape Breton), who brought forth the conceptual approach of "two-eyed seeing" in ecological research. It reminds us of the importance to see the subject through both a mainstream ecological lens or eye as well as through a cultural Mi'kmaw lens for the benefit of all. We are guided to see from both perspectives without one eye overpowering the other. Many times in our collaborative ecological work we must embark on a co-learning journey as this weaving of perspectives and worldviews is not always a clear path ahead. We give thanks to Albert as well as colleagues Cheryl Bartlett and Annamarie Hatcher from Cape Breton University who have promoted this concept for over a decade.

Through my conservation work in Kespukwitk (Southwest Nova Scotia) i have been able to refer to Etuaptmumk as a way to include Mi'kmaw ways of knowing, learning, and recovering rare species. It was Albert's voice that my non-Mi'kmaw colleagues heard and accepted this potentially intellectually challenging mission with great heart. I thank Albert for making a path for young researchers like me in order to do the Two-eyed Seeing work.

The Marshalls' Journey to Find Muin's Story

For over 20 years the late Mi'kmaw Elder Lillian Marshall from Potlotek, Unama'ki (Chapel Island, Cape Breton), worked to revive the old story, Muin aqq Luiknek Te'sijik Ntuksuinuk (Bear and the Seven Bird Hunters). Passed through various means over the generations, including being transcribed by Stansbury Hagar in 1900, this story was more than a teaching about time-keeping through watching constellations. For Lillian, it also carried meaning and clues about the ancient custom of the Mid-Winter Feast. Rekindling both the story and the feast ceremony is attributed to Elder Lillian.

In 2007 Cheryl Bartlett, a researcher with Cape Breton University's Integrative Science Program, met with Jim Hesser, the Canadian Chair of the International Year of Astronomy (2009), and Mi'kmaw Elders to discuss highlighting a Mi'kmaw night sky story for the year-long celebration. It was then that Elder Lillian spoke of this Muin story and all of the work flowed from there. The late Elder Murdena Marshall from Eskasoni, Unama'ki, joined the research effort as did Prune Harris, Sana Kavanagh, and Kristy Read. They were instrumental in talking through many variations of this story's teachings to capture the most effective narrative to publish in a book and present on the world's stage in 2009. *Muin aqq L'uiknek te'sijik Ntuksuinu'k / Muin and the Seven Bird Hunters* was published and a video was created. This story has continued to find new tellers and voices over the past decade.

We are all grateful to the late Elders Lillian Marshall and Murdena Marshall for working tirelessly for our Mi'kmaw communities and next generations. I am a beneficiary of their work. I am honoured to have been given the blessing from Elder Albert Marshall to share my own version of this story within this book and play.

Melissa Sue Labrador "Doah Aye Nibi"

Visual artist Melissa Sue Labrador is from the Wildcat Community in South Brookfield, Nova Scotia. Commenting on her art for this book cover she says, "I wanted to represent the two views strongly, but also represent the natural world and the creatures (chimney swifts) that become a bridge to two different worldviews – how Nature plays a role in everyone's life and has a way of showing us we are all connected."

She is the daughter of well-known and award-winning Mi'kmaq-style birchbark canoe builder Todd G. Labrador and the late spiritual leader, artist, and knowledge-keeper Jean Augustine-McIsaac, and granddaughter of the late Elder/Hereditary Chief of the Acadia First Nation, Charles W. Labrador. Melissa's childhood was spent immersed in Mi'kmaw culture, and traditional values and ways.

Melissa currently works with birch bark by making bowls and containers, winter bark etchings, and by assisting her father with the creation of his canoes. Inspiration for her painting stems from her close upbringing to the sacred sites of Kejimkujik and surrounding areas. She continues to study and work with the ancient rock carvings of her Ancestors to better understand the ways of her people and the intensity and importance of her culture.

Melissa promotes and shares traditional ecological knowledge and traditional plant medicine k
nowledge. Her voice has become an echo of her upbringing in her grandfather's footsteps, as she brings awareness to the disrespect that Nova Scotia forests, waters, and animals are feeling, and she promotes the vision that we all must view Mother Earth as a living being for the sake of our future – our children.

She currently resides in the Wildcat Community where she home-schools her twins.

shalan joudry

shalan joudry is an oral storyteller, poet, ecologist, and mother from the traditional district of Kespukwitk (Southwest Nova Scotia). She lives and works in her community of L'sitkuk (Bear River First Nation) with her family. There she works seasonally as a cultural interpreter and ecologist, while dedicating much of her time to artistic projects and events, touring her unique modern storytelling. Using her theatrical background, shalan brings Mi'kmaw stories to a new generation of listeners, as well as recounting personally crafted narratives that follow Mi'kmaw storying custom.

With support through Arts Nova Scotia and Two Planks and a Passion Theatre, shalan wrote this play in the winter of 2018 for its stage production by the theatre company in Canning, Nova Scotia. Her literary writing has appeared in journals and anthologies. Shalan's first book of poetry, *Generations Re-merging* was published by Gaspereau Press in 2014. Of both Mi'kmaw and European ancestry, shalan weaves worldviews in ecology and her writing.